ALL THE FOOTPRINTS I LEFT WERE RED

Rowena Knight was born in 1988 in Palmerston North, New Zealand, but moved to England on her thirteenth birthday. She is a graduate of Durham University, where she founded the poetry society. Her poetry was commended in the Foyle Young Poets of the Year Award in 2006, has been twice longlisted in the Mslexia Poetry Competition, and was shortlisted for the Jane Martin Poetry Prize in 2015. Her work has appeared in many magazines and journals, including *Magma*, *Cadaverine Magazine*, *The Rialto*, and *Cake*. *All the Footprints I Left Were Red* is her first pamphlet.

All the Footprints
I Left Were Red

R O W E N A   K N I G H T

Valley Press

First published in 2016 by Valley Press
Woodend, The Crescent, Scarborough, YO11 2PW
www.valleypressuk.com

First edition, first printing (July 2016)

ISBN 978-1-908853-75-2
Cat. no. VP0092

Printed and bound in Great Britain by
Charlesworth Press, Wakefield

Contents

In memory of Mrs McKendry,
a teacher like no other

Made.com

I ordered a couch with slender legs, soft
as a girl, with the feel of an earlobe
or peach. The colour of cream
left out, a cat's tongue lapping the light.

A couch for buttered Sundays, smooth white wine,
for leaving bills to crinkle and yellow.
A couch for entertaining Marcia,
for her gold legs to unfold and open.

Imagine my horror when I tugged free
the last piece to find a woman, flat-packed
at the back. Polished and white as a sink,
she's hat-stand tall, and doesn't say a word.

She's quite the thing next to the piano,
one arm half-raised, as if about to speak.

Fictions

You never lost your mind,
not completely, simply forgot it on occasion
down the side of the bed,
on the kitchen table.
Soap in the mouths of little girls
and all our furniture sold.

I strip photographs, searching for claws.
A beating in the clasp of your hand, a shout
at the crease of your smile.
Your skin is smooth. I hate you for it;
the halo of curls, kind eyes.

Let there be a hint of coarse hair,
a curse coiled on your tongue.
Laughter is no use to me:
give me a bottle in your hand,
or at least, a balled fist.

I'll swallow such cliché more readily
than that handsome man in his wedding suit,
piggy backs, the photo of you
fixing an angel on the Christmas tree.

Flotation

The wind rubs my mother's skin
as she and her sisters hurtle

up and down, feet slapping the decks,
trailing their screams like balloons,

three girls who've never known collision.
Neighbours and rules

are things of dry land, of England.
She hasn't been scolded for days,

her parents too seasick and dazed
by the scale of their decision,

the years stacked into boxes
of crockery and photographs.

Sequinned with pool water
she's oblivious to her NHS glasses,

the knees she has yet to grow into,
the twenty-somethings who lean

into each other in the rich dark
of the bar, cupping their cocktails

as though they've forgotten
they're holding anything.

Two weeks in and she's mastered floating.
She's consuming the library's limited collection

and embroidering a runner
for a dressing table she has yet to own.

She avoids the staff,
their wiry beards and sunburn.

In the creaking dining room
she hears women weigh

each man's flaws and merits
in low voices. *The Greeks,*

the women call them. She cuts her tongue
on brittle parcels of pastry;

the Greeks like to introduce their guests
to exotic foods. For her sister's birthday

they present a palatial cake.
Acid-yellow and cold it slips

down her throat like a slug.
Her mother heaves it overboard

when she thinks no-one's looking.
The sea accepts it without question.

Later, as the sun streams
through her new blue world,

she will watch the porpoises thread
their silver bodies through the waves.

In the disco she'll request "Dancing Queen",
as she does every night,

and dance like a girl who hasn't known
the sobriety of land,

as she never danced in Liverpool
and never will again.

The Daughters

The escapologist's daughter is larger than he would like.
He has put her on a diet and locked the cupboard.

The astronomer's daughter is picked out in stars.
She is waiting for someone to label her constellation.

The architect's daughter leans on one foot,
her body has too many angles.

The musician's daughter refuses to sing
though he knows her voice would be the perfect accompaniment.

The chef's daughter eats ketchup with everything
and never apologises.

The plumber's daughter weeps
and he cannot stop her tears.

So many women without names;
eternal girls with mirrored faces.
When their fathers leave the room they forget who they are.

One day, if they are lucky, they will become wives,
then mothers to such men.
They wear possessive apostrophes around their necks like
    pendants.

Valuables

He's no more than a thief, with an eye
for a cracked window, a lock with its tongue

withdrawn. Her story shrinks beneath tuts.
They'd shared a bottle of wine,

dirty jokes. She was a purse
in a back pocket, a door ticking on a breeze.

He's at her favourite coffee shop.
He takes buses, goes clubbing.

She stays in. Showers.
Her skin tautens to leather.

When she unzips her lips pennies
come pouring out. No one will stoop

to collect their bad luck.

Foreign

There should be so much more than this:
paper bags from the dairy,
pebbly with sugar. Snatches
of waiata. Bare feet on wood,
grit dusting. Disembodied water.

But child doesn't care for culture
or weather. Bonfires and beaches
were backdrop, kea and kakapo
only radio. I would have pendulumed
into the river again and again.

My mother fed me strictly
on Enid Blyton till my head
became a conker, my eyes
penny sweets. I thought the English
drank only lemonade, always

wore macs and wellies,
and that it was the foreign in me
that made me strange and friendless.
My mother forbade eating in public,
foul language, her bedroom.

I wore Peter Pan collars to church
and dreamt of an island of mothers,
a refuge from awkward barbecues,
her perpetual homesickness.
I wanted to cure her of herself,

solve the puzzle of the word "blazer".
We left. I learned it; an unrelenting,
polyester clinch, coffin-black.
I was too old for conker fights,
for Enid. My schoolbag didn't bear

the tick of approval and it wasn't
the English in me, it wasn't one country
but all. I kept my words.
Lollies, togs, gumboots, bach.
A spell to take me back.

dairy: newsagent
waiata: the Māori word for song
kea and *kakapo*: native New Zealand birds
lollies: sweets
togs: swimming costume
gumboots: wellington boots
bach: beach house

Heaven

started as a promise, a trip to a mall-coddled Santa, a post-injection lollipop. When I opened my illustrated Bible gold pillars rose from its pages and disappeared into a crown of cloud. The book decayed, spine shrinking in a mess of filmy stitches, but heaven shone bright as a dollar.

Each night I prayed for dreams of Jesus or Santa, a saviour from witches with spoons and tricks. I prayed for my mother's homesick heart; to be a pastel girl with an appetite for reality TV. For sun-coloured colonnades, and a dad who doesn't leave.

At thirteen I took a plane and got closer to it. Thirty hours of white light trapped above corrugated clouds. A new country meant a new girl, a skirt in a herd of uniforms. I would eat *Big Brother*, backpacks the colour of lip gloss, and hair ties in the shape of fruit. My mother wouldn't cry, back in her world of soft vowels and perfect queues.

And then the questions came, along with stiff black polyester and *Why do you talk like that?* Question marks hooked into skin, burrowed and bred at night in piles of dirty white shirts. Cracks in the ceiling, borer in the bedroom, a spanner in the belly's works. I took a closer look at god

and he was tinsel, a twenty-cent piece slipped under a pillow. And mean, with his gavel, his silly beard spewing curls. I didn't want him to stuff sweets up my sleeves and send me back to my mother, I wanted him to give me a reason, to tell me why all she said was one day, we'll die and go to heaven. Borer in the brain, tiny black eclipses in the amygdala.

Like a witch he shrank until only a red velvet hat remained, a ridiculous trinket in a food court, and heaven a mall pretending we need it. Giving up stopped being a bad thing, I could lie down in a box like a pair of shoes and let someone slot me into the earth. All that cool soil, damp like a mother's kiss. And the insects, taking what they need and carrying it out into the world.

borer: woodworm

The Goblin Queen

Tired of being maternal and chaste
I abandon my brother's name, cry out instead
for the goblin king. He stops mid-serenade,
drops to my side. We make love right there
in the Escher room as staircases drift by.

Toby is happy here, with his gnarled companions.
They never bore of playing with him,
sing lullabies of snails and voodoo,
thunder and lightning. Two incipient nubs
at his temples tell me he is turning.

For a year, everything is magic.
I play at princess, applying lipstick in my tower room.
Jareth conjures the dress I wore in a dream;
I think I'll never take it off. He brings me liquid globes,
little portals to my old life.

At first I watch the search, my father's face
glazed with tears on TV appeals.
My stepmother's mouth a delicious twist of pain.
Grim-faced police lead dogs through the park where once
I rehearsed the words only a child could know by heart.

Another year passes. Jareth declares
the castle grounds forbidden. Never takes me
to the ballroom, sings only occasionally; the same songs,
on repeat. He says he was unprepared
for my capitulation. He is a terrible liar.

I tire of his crystal gifts. The goblins build
a display cabinet for them; they are good with their hands,
less so with conversation. I spy on old friends
as they swap ghost stories at sleepovers.
Their clumsy first kisses.

He turns owl more often. Bang
of the clock, shuffle of wings, then he's gone
all night. I give up asking where he goes,
or what happened to forever.
Yesterday I caught him gazing at a bauble

with the face of a fortune-teller.
It held a teenage girl; head-of-drama-club type,
all black leggings, artistic hair.
I unbutton the dress,
find my jeans folded neatly in a chest.

I slip out the back entrance
– the way the worm kept from me –
past the guards, and home. My room exactly
as I left it. I run to the dressing table
and call on old friends.

The mirror offers a silent reply:
a woman with feathered hair,
straining skin, and goblin eyes.

Angel Beach

He cracked my eyes awake when I was thirteen.
Epiphany hot and sweet as December,
sand light as prayers
stuck to feet, navel, hair.
The sky opened like an eye,
left me dizzy. We pocketed shells
for offerings, had our Coke communion.
The beach sang with us,
the bach an untuned guitar
full of praise. Hands warm and heavy
as sun on my back
as we collected each other's tears.
Enough salt water to fill a horizon with faith,
to swim in its green.
We were sure the feathers that spined our feet
were left by angels,
that even the ringing song of frogs
was a repetition of His name.

Jonathan

We knew that he was dying
but it was a hazy kind of knowing.
We continued to tussle over the handlebars
of his wheelchair, parade his smile proudly
around the playground. We knew
the trails of silver coins spelling out his name
would save him; we had faith in their magic.
There was no place for death,
no colour crayon to draw him with.
He didn't fit in our lunchboxes,
we whipped him away with skipping ropes,
sealed his eyes with glitter glue.

Our spells failed. Death stepped across our
ten-cent hopes, scattered the carefully
constructed letters. Jonathan shrunk
to a thin shrub, frail green thumbnails of leaves,
and only a tiny white plaque to remind us.
And the memory of crying on the classroom carpet
as the hometime songs were sung,
his clumsy embrace, kiss on my cheek.

Earlobes

I've promised to pay more attention to earlobes,
those swan-soft tabs, the only parts of us
that remain infant.

Will you join me? Will you loop your earrings
from their holes, will you tie up your hair

and taking yourself solemnly by the ear,
swear never to forget that two small parts of you
will not harden to a walnut's wrinkle,

but will always give way to the thumb's curious strum,
a lover's wandering lips?

Learning to Love a Vegetarian

You return from the grocer's
with straining bags, flushed and content
as though we'd just made love.

I wonder if you'll ever undress me
with as much relish as you ease an onion
from its papery skin,
or hold me as tenderly as you hold
a portobello mushroom.

You sigh with pleasure as you slice,
loving the silhouette's swell.
I suspect my figure will never compare,
and I probably can't satisfy you
like a hearty lentil casserole,
or spice your eyes with tears
the way a good onion does
(is it the pain, or the beauty?).

But I am set on your artichoke heart, love,
so I steal a can of your beloved kidney beans,
take a wet, forbidden fistful
and leave a trail
from the kitchen,
up the stairs,
into your bedroom.
Sprawl naked on the bed,
a red jewel
in my mouth,
my navel.

Garlic

you will never
make me cry,
unlike your onion cousin,
the prick

who sends me pink
and cringing to my room.
Peppery pearl mellowed
in the saucepan's cradle,

you make yourself known
in kinder ways, your geodes
treasure to the tongue.
I love to undress you –

snapping each back
with the flat
of my blade, unpeeling
wafery layers, leaving you

cleanly naked.
My fingers heart the shine
and squeak of you.
Friendly thumb,

savoury nub,
generously you spill
your pungence and lodge
beneath the nail's roof.

Sweetened seed,
little spiced moon,
all evening I'll taste
the shock of you.

Recipes politely request
a clove, or two, but I need
a fistful, the whole
of the heart's fruit.

Scar

You take each step deliberately
as though pressing your foot

to a sewing machine's pedal,
your thoughts precise as needlework.

I've observed each of your facial expressions
(surprise is the wide sky of your forehead,

love a slight smile that settles in your face
like a cat onto a bed),

but I can't recall your face
folding into a frown.

You do not worry that the wind's hand
will turn your damp hair haphazard,

or dream that you're naked and sitting an exam
on the mating habits of dinosaurs.

While I scurry eyeliner across my lid
and flay my duvet for the music of keys,

you are always on time.
But one night you were

bone and salt water
in my arms, and I kissed your forehead

as though the scar there
were no more than a target for my lips.

Red

Today I stepped on a heart.
The heel of my shoe
punctured the taut muscle –
I couldn't dam the gurgling blood.

They tell me it isn't my fault.
People shouldn't leave their hearts
out in the open like that, they should know
that girls like me are focused on our destinations
and can't pay attention to our feet.

But it's hard to forget.
On my way home
all the footprints I left were red.

How to Not Save a Drowning Spider

Turn away from the frantic ballet,
a clutch of eyelashes
pummelled in circles. Look instead
at the tealights framing the garden.
Busy yourself arranging chairs.
Spear cubes of cheese and pineapple.

It is caught now, anyway,
in the tap's surge and choir.
Its legs, once graceful
embroidery needles,
scrabble for a foothold.

Don't. Not this time.
Death is not an event,
least of all for the tiny
glossy abdomens
snickering over earth.

You are no longer the girl who plucked snails
from the pavement's thoroughfare.
Consider the strawberries
bleeding sweetness into air.
Note the potato salad, how white
its upturned scalps.

Leave the paddling pool.
Don't go fishing for that dark star,
lifting it to the surface
like a child sifting seawater.

Bath Poem

She spends an indecent amount of time in the bath
emerging only to write poems
about being in the bath.

When her fingers turn to soft walnuts
she knows it is time to press them to the keyboard.
She has determined the ratio of water to word.

There is always bubble bath, of course.
She writes of how it pearls her breasts.
She might even mention the dark triangle of her "sex".

Her poems don't mention the mould
congregating in ceiling corners.
She never slits a swatch from her knee whilst shaving.

She is committed to the art of the bath poem:
always naked, always clean,
waiting for you like a peach.

Acknowledgements

I would like to thank: Nicole and Helen, for being such dedicated "fans"; Tamar Yoseloff and the Routes family, for their support and insightful critique; the Durham University Poetry Society (especially Jamie, Jan, John, Josie, Matthew, and Reetta) for their encouragement and showing me that writing needn't be a solitary activity; Catherine Smith, for her sage teaching and inspiring me with her neverending joy in writing; Kate Potts, for being so generous with her time and views; Carmina Masoliver and the *She Grrrowls* crew, for opportunities to share my work and encounter other fantastic poets; Tim Wells, for his no-nonsense critique and helping me showcase my work; my family, especially my mother for sharing her stories; and Kayo, for insisting that I was good enough.

The following poems, or earlier versions, have previously appeared elsewhere:
Angelic Dynamo – 'Earlobes'
Astronaut Zine – 'Bath Poem'
Bare Fiction – 'Flotation'
Cadaverine Magazine – 'Jonathan'
Magma – 'Foreign'
Seasick Blue: Poems from the Tower Poetry Summer School 2008 – 'Angel Beach'
The Morning Star – 'Valuables'
The Rialto – 'Made.com'
Silkworms Ink – 'Learning to Love a Vegetarian'
'Heaven' was commissioned by Kate Potts for Roddy Lumsden's *Discomfort Zone II* event.

Finally, I would like to thank the Foyle Foundation and the Poetry Society for a commendation in the Foyle Young Poet of the Year Award, which was instrumental early in my writing career.